NAKITTA CLEGG FOXX

A 21-Day Journal to Faith, Freedom & Forward Movement

Foreword by Dr. Mia Knight Wright

DEDICATION

To the three men in my life who I will always cherish…

My dad, Theodis Clegg. He was a man of great wisdom. I'd love to hear his thoughts on these entries and what his journal entry would be for each one.

Keep resting, Dad
4.18.1945 – 6.27.1991

My brother, Byron Patrick Clegg. You actually started this morning inspiration thing. We wake up many mornings to your routine of seeking God and sharing with us. Even through your struggles you remain consistent. I'm proud of you, and I love you!

My son, **Ace Maddox Foxx**. Everything I do is for and inspired by you and your sister. But as a man, I want this to inspire and challenge you to read, pay attention to details and be expressive on your journey. Keep being amazing, Son. I love you!

FOREWORD

"Early in the morning, my soul shall rise to thee."

I remember singing this hymn as a child. I doubt that I had any real understanding of the power rooted in an early encounter with God or what meeting God in the morning actually meant for the life of the believer.

Poet and songwriter Reginald Heber penned the deeply devotional Christian hymn "Holy, Holy, Holy! Lord God Almighty" in 1826. Even today, the lyrics still challenge each believer to connect with God before the day becomes filled with life's distractions. It is in God's presence that we gain clarity, direction, and peace for each day's journey.

Much like Reginald Heber, Nakitta Foxx is a gifted songstress, poet, and author who seeks to infuse the atmosphere with God's anointing. She is a worshipper at heart—an instrument and vessel for God's use and glory.

Now we have the opportunity to come closer to her journey, be inspired, and be challenged to live closer to God through devotion and action. Just as Heber sought to introduce more poetic hymns into the traditional church of his time, Nakitta now encourages people everywhere to connect deeply through intentional time set aside to meet God.

I am inspired by her writings, reflections, and challenges, and I believe you will be too. Twenty-one days of devotion and intention can lead to a lifetime of change and blessing.

So let me encourage you to join Nakitta on this journey and see what God will do!

Dr. Mia Knight Wright
Co-Pastor, The Fountain of Praise

 Intro

There's nothing like the start of a brand new day. The sun rising. The birds chirping in the trees. The faint sounds of cars and buses going down the street. The hot mug of coffee (or tea) resting on the kitchen table. Yes, it's the simple things we often overlook because, for many of us, our mornings look a little different.

We may find ourselves hitting the snooze button several times before we decide to get up, rushing late to work because we overslept, still having to get the kids ready for school—faces washed, teeth brushed, hair combed and clothes ready to wear—all the while woofing down a quick breakfast to settle our cravings. Then, we find ourselves fighting rush hour traffic to reach our destinations and the list goes on and on and on.

We become so busy with our morning routines that we lack the time to center ourselves and command our day before it even starts. As a mom, friend, sister, daughter, worship leader and artist, I know firsthand what it's like to feel stretched. You're pulled in so many different directions fulfilling so many different obligations that, just like a rubberband, overtime the tension becomes too much. You begin to break. Snap. Pop.

Good Morning. was birthed out of one of my breaking points. I had reached a very dark place in my life where I needed light. I needed to heal. I needed more peace, more clarity, more God. I realized that, if anything in my life was going to change, it had to start at the beginning of my day. So, I made a decision that before I answered to the world, I would answer to God.

I started a routine where I would wake up early in the morning and ask God, "What do You want to say to me today? How do You want me to think? How do You want me to move?" And in the stillness of those moments, He met me each and every time. He poured wisdom into my spirit, taken from my life experiences. I hope it will empower you to know that you have everything you need to get through and make it in life. We can do all things through Christ who strengthens us! (Philippians 4:13)

I chose 21 days because I've always heard the saying, "21 days build a habit." Anything worth doing is worth making it a habit, and studies show that habits form—whether good or bad—after 21 days of consistent effort.

Each morning, I want you to read, reflect, write and rise to the occasion. I believe God is going to do a new thing in you, but you've got to put in the work. Work for the change you seek so that this new habit becomes a lifestyle.

Now, let me be clear. I'll be the first to admit that I do not have it all figured out. I don't claim to know it all nor do I live a picture-perfect life. I am still a work-in-progress. This journal is not all about me; it's about us walking this journey together, showing up daily and trusting God through every high and low as life keeps lifin.'

So as the sun rises over these next 21 days, I believe something powerful will rise within you too--greater faith, deeper confidence in God, renewed strength and an unstoppable momentum toward the life He has already prepared for you.

Yes, it's a new day on the horizon, and I'm excited about what's yet to unfold! This is your new beginning. This is your reset. This is your moment. How you start your day is how you shape it.

Rise and shine!

Challenge Yourself

Some mornings, I honestly don't know what I struggle with the most—waking up extra early for my devotional time or staying committed to my daily workout routine. On the days I don't have to be up early or transport the kids to and from school, I want to bury myself in my covers and sleep in as long as I can. No alarm clocks. No morning meetings. No agenda. Just the deep, uninterrupted rest my body so desperately needs because I am tyeeeed. (Translation: tired)

But as I lay here contemplating my next move, a simple but powerful thought moves me to action. *If you don't challenge yourself, then how will you ever change?* Wow! That one question shifts everything.

It's during our moments of hesitation and resistance that we have to push ourselves to greater. Yes, it's easy to retreat and do nothing. Some days, I just don't want to do it. But if I don't push myself beyond my feelings and emotions, then I'll never grow beyond them. Change requires movement, and movement often begins when we decide to rise in the middle of resistance.

I can definitely see the difference a morning of intentional devotion makes in my day. When I start my morning in the Word, listening for God's voice and meditating on His truth, something shifts inside of me. My mindset changes. My mood improves. My focus sharpens. It's as if that quiet time cranks up the engine of my day, giving me the energy and clarity to accomplish more than I ever do than on the mornings when I sneak in extra sleep.

Listen, I'm learning that, if you never push yourself mentally or physically, you will never see the potential of who you can become or how far you can go. Comfort may feel good in the moment, but comfort keeps you stagnant. Challenge is what creates change, and I am reminded of this lesson every single time I step into the gym.

During those workouts—whew—it's *tuff*! Yes, I said *tuff* just like the kids say. The weights are heavy. I'm tired out of my mind. My muscles are sore, and I can

Good Morning.

barely move. But as I begin to see my body transform little by little, it encourages me to keep going back for more. The pain has a purpose, and the progress is real! No more complaints from me.

The changes I need to see sometimes come with challenging myself to do things that may feel uncomfortable, inconvenient or even hurt. But just like building muscle, we have to keep flexing and stretching ourselves in order to increase our capacity. And if we remain consistent, especially on the hard days, we will begin to see the evidence of our efforts in real time.

So get up now and don't let comfort keep you from your calling. Challenge yourself. Because at the end of the day, no one else can take the steps for you. Only you can move you. Chef's kiss.

Good Morning.

Reflect

Hebrews 12:11 No discipline seems pleasant at the time, but painful. Later on, however, it produces a harvest of righteousness and peace for those who have been trained by it.

Romans 12:2 Do not conform to the pattern of this world, but be transformed by the renewing of your mind. Then you will be able to test and approve what God's will is—his good, pleasing and perfect will.

Today, I will challenge myself to...

Stay Focused

Why do you think you're constantly being thrown lemons? Everything is supposed to be sweet and light, right? But, if only life was that simple, it would be a bed of roses. When challenges keep showing up, it's often because there's something valuable inside of you worth protecting. Even roses bear thorns.

We all hold so much significant value within God's kingdom that the enemy sends daily distractions to try and derail us. Honestly speaking, there have been many times I've allowed things to distract me and shift my focus.

How many times have you delayed your calling because you were worried about something that didn't truly matter?

We have to recognize those moments when they occur—when our focus begins to drift. We must be ever so careful to avoid the snares and traps of the enemy by making sure we are staying connected to God and are mindful of our behaviors. Maintaining a laser-like focus on God and self will help to ensure we aren't swaying too far off course.

Sometimes being focused requires being selfish, and that doesn't have to be a bad thing. There is a way to be about yourself without slighting others. The ones who genuinely support you will understand the time and care YOU need during this season. Don't be the one who's always motivating and helping others resolve their problems that you neglect your own.

Staying focused may look small in the moment, but that single step can grow into something beautiful. Getting in one door could be the key to opening soooo many others!

Stay focused and finish the course. Run your own race at your own pace. Don't be sidetracked by what appears to look good for you but is really working against you.

Pray and stay disciplined. There's nothing more rewarding than enjoying the

Good Morning.

fruits of your labor because you decided to stay focused on what God placed in your heart.

Good Morning.

Reflect

Psalm 119:12 Praise be to you, LORD; teach me your decrees.

Proverbs 4:25-26 Let your eyes look straight ahead; fix your gaze directly before you. Give careful thought to the paths for your feet and be steadfast in all your ways.

Romans 8:5 Those who live according to the flesh have their minds set on what the flesh desires; but those who live in accordance with the Spirit have their minds set on what the Spirit desires.

Today, I will focus on...

Run With It!

During my quiet time this morning, I looked over my vision and all my plans for the year, and I'll have to admit that I'm super excited! There are many great things I am striving to accomplish. Some goals are a repeat from previous years. Others are brand new, stretching me into new territory. But all of them require one thing—intention.

I've learned that vision becomes powerful the moment it leaves your mind and meets paper. Writing it down gives it structure. Whatever your goals are I encourage you to put them on paper.

Although some may seem small and trivial and play a minor part initially, still write them down. Include timelines, what you want it to look like, who you want it to impact, where you want it to occur, and as many other details you can think of. The more you can begin to see it, the quicker you are to seize it and run with it.

Why "run with it?" I'm glad you asked. You see, it's easy to write things down on paper. We can write volumes of goals for any and everything under the sun. Yet, those goals are meaningless without putting in some work behind them.

Think of it this way. You can create a grocery list and know all what you need to maintain your household. But until you actually go to the grocery store, gather the listed items and pay for them, your grocery list has limited value. It's a great start, but it cannot feed you. Ink without action is just decoration.

As the Bible says, faith without works is dead. Therefore, manifestation requires movement. Put legs to those thoughts and dreams. Don't just let them sit there on paper.

In the scripture that talks about writing the vision and making it plain, there is a subsequent clause—"That he may run who reads it." Remember, your vision is not just for you but for others too. It cannot move anyone if it hasn't first moved you.

Good Morning.

So whatever the dream, whatever the vision, write it clearly and make it plain. Then, tighten up your discipline, set your focus and run with it!

Good Morning.

Reflect

Habakkuk 2:2 Then the LORD replied: "Write down the revelation and make it plain on tablets so that a herald may run with it."

What is your vision for this year?
Today, I'm activating my vision by...

Faith It Out

All last night, while I was asleep, I could hear myself subconsciously telling myself, "Aht Aht…Aht Aht…No wavering! No wavering!" Then, I woke up this morning with a reminder for you.

A lot of times we pray for things believing God will answer our prayers until doubt, fear and worry begin to creep in. It's like we know He's going to resolve the issue, but then we begin to think about the what-ifs.

What if the money really doesn't come? What if the diagnosis gets worse? What if the interview was all a joke? What if this relationship doesn't work out? What if I fail?

Within a matter of moments, our faith goes from 100 to 0 when it should have gone the other way around. If we're not walking in faith, then we're walking in fear, and just an inkling of fear can overtake us.

As I've often heard, fear is really *false evidence appearing real*. All the negative outcomes we think could happen never really do.

The word of God tells us that He has not given us a spirit of fear but of love, power and a sound mind (2 Timothy 1:7). That means when fear shows up, it's not coming from Him, and we don't have to accept it. When we feel defeat approaching, we must activate our faith. We must remind ourselves WHO we are and WHOSE we are and have complete trust in it.

Every day, we put our faith in a lot of things without even thinking about it. How many times do we inspect our chairs and couches before we sit down? We're not afraid they are going to fall apart when we sit down on them. We don't cautiously test whether they will hold us. We just sit down and sometimes not so gently— fully expecting them to support our weight.

This is the same kind of faith we should have in God. We have to believe and trust that what He says to us and about us is true and apply it to our everyday lives.

Good Morning.

Think His Word. Speak His Word. Believe His Word. Trust His Word.

I'm going to plop down (as the elders would say) on His promises with no care or second thought because I'm confident He has me! Increasing my level of faith requires a deeper knowing, deeper trust, which God dealt with me on yesterday, and a stronger commitment to staying the course—confident, secure and unbothered.

No matter the circumstances, we simply have to faith it out. No wavering. No retreating. No rehearsing fear.

If we have the blind faith to sit in chairs confidently, why can't we trust God the same? All things are working together for our good—even when we can't see it yet!

Good Morning.

Luke 1:37 For no word from God will ever fail.

2 Corinthians 5:7 For we live by faith, not by sight.

Hebrews 11:1 Now faith is confidence in what we hope for and assurance about what we do not see.

Today, I trust God to...

Day 5

Embrace the Process

This morning, I woke up wondering and asking God, "Does anyone else go through the things I go through?" I'm a huge fan of roller coasters, but I know I didn't sign up for all the dips, turns and unexpected loops on this ride called life. Whew chile!

And you want to know what God said to me? He asked, "Did any of it kill you? Did you finish a little stronger, wiser and even better perhaps?" Wow! That stopped me in my tracks.

Every day that felt like life was knocking me down, I still found the strength to stand back up. Every challenge that tried to break me only revealed something greater within me. I know there are days you feel like you are facing a playground bully. Right? But you must remember that everything meaningful has a process.

If you think about it, pressure produces superior results as well as beauty. Let's look at a diamond for example. The result of what you see didn't start that way. It took extreme heat and intense pressure over long periods of time deep beneath the earth to form this beautiful jewel.

So I couldn't help but compare myself to a diamond. I've been in some extremely heated situations and under some intense pressure—financial droughts, relationship drama, health challenges, court cases, etc. Some days, I wondered if I would even make it through the day. But I refused to quit.

I stayed the course and decided I would embrace the process—not as punishment but as a pathway to purpose. And every time I overcame another challenge, I shined a little brighter. My vision became clearer, and my strength grew deeper.

The human side of us doesn't wake up asking for conflict, adversity or struggle. Most of us would gladly choose a smooth, drama-free path through life. But when life starts lifin', we must remember that some of our greatest victories can emerge from our toughest defeats.

Good Morning.

Those difficult moments aren't detours. They're part of the design. They are the refining fires that prepare us for purpose. So instead of fighting the process, embrace it!

Today, whenever I face a new challenge, I ask myself, "How will this make me stronger, better and wiser?" The road ahead may twist, dip or even turn when I least expect it, but I'm no longer afraid of the ride.

I know every turn, every test and every ounce of pressure is shaping something powerful within me. And like a diamond formed under pressure, I'm coming out of it all with a shine that can't be dimmed. Alexa, play Rihanna's *Shine Bright like a Diamond*.

Good Morning.

1 Peter 1:7 These have come so that the proven genuineness of your faith—of greater worth than gold, which perishes even though refined by fire—may result in praise, glory and honor when Jesus Christ is revealed.

Isaiah 48:10 See I have refined you, though not as silver; I have tested you in the furnace of affliction.

James 1:2-4 Consider it pure joy, my brothers and sisters, whenever you face trials of many kinds, because you know that the testing of your faith produces perseverance. Let perseverance finish its work so that you may be mature and complete, not lacking anything.

Today, I embrace the fact that...

Fix the Broken Places

This morning, after dropping my kids off, my car flashed a warning signal. One of my tires had dropped to 0% air pressure. I immediately headed to my usual tire shop to see if it could be inflated or patched. After checking the tire, the technician told me that the previous patch was busted and couldn't be repaired again. I would need a brand-new tire. He said I could still make it to *Discount Tire* and further explained that, although the tire was damaged, it was still "doable."

Hmmnnn. That made me stop and reflect. How many of us are living life exactly like that tire—damaged but still doing? How far do we think we can progress in anything when we are operating as damaged vessels? If we don't address the problem, we risk causing harm not only to ourselves but to those around us.

I know the phrase "broken crayons still color" is popular, and I've even said it myself. While it's true, it made me think about how there are functioning drug addicts and alcoholics—people who are "doing" but still deeply damaged.

Just because we're still able to function doesn't mean we shouldn't focus on fixing the broken places in our lives. Using our ability to keep going as an excuse to avoid healing can be dangerous. We simply need to fix the broken places.

The first step towards repair is acknowledgement. We must be honest enough with ourselves to admit that something within us needs attention. Ignoring the cracks does not make them disappear nor does pretending everything is alright bring about healing. We must first say to ourselves, "This here needs to get fixed."

Once we acknowledge the broken areas, we must give ourselves permission to pause and reflect. Let's sit back and take the time to think about it. Too often, we rush through life carrying unresolved wounds. Life has a way of keeping us busy. We move from responsibility to responsibility, task to task, goal to goal, never taking the time to examine what's been damaged along the way. True healing requires us to slow down long enough to examine the areas that need repair.

Good Morning.

Another important step in repairing the broken places is releasing what contributed to the damage. Sometimes our brokenness comes from people who mistreated us or the painful circumstances beyond our control.

Other times, it comes from the choices we made while doing the best we could with what we knew to do at the time. Regardless of the source, true healing begins when we release the bitterness, regret and the exhausting habit of replaying the past. Holding onto those things only keeps the wound open.

Let's be honest. We've got work to do, and it won't just happen overnight. It is important for us to realize that restoration is a process, not a moment. Some areas of our lives may heal quickly, while others require patience, intention and consistent effort. The key is to remain committed to the work of becoming whole.

I've been working on me for quite some time now, and I love the progress I am making. I refuse to keep patching up my hurt and brokenness with excuses, avoidance or neglect. I'm choosing to face those areas head-on and do the work required for real healing. The strongest part of our story is not defined by what was broken. It is defined by our willingness to repair, rebuild and rise again.

Good Morning.

Revelation 21:5 He who was seated on the throne said, "I am making everything new!" Then he said, "Write this down, for these words are trustworthy and true."

Reflect

Isaiah 40:29 He gives strength to the weary and increases the power of the weak.

Psalm 147:3 He heals the brokenhearted and binds up their wounds.

Joel 2:25 I will repay you for the years the locusts have eaten —the great locust and the young locust, the other locusts and the locust swarm—my great army that I sent among you.

Today, I will work on fixing...

____

____

____

____

____

____

Forgive & Release

I want you to be free this morning. Not halfway free nor the pretending-to-be-okay free. I'm talking about the kind of freedom that allows you to breathe without the weight of yesterday pressing against your chest. Forgive. And let it go!

Release the hurt, the pain, the resentment and animosity caused by others. You don't have to rest in that anymore. Yes, it may have happened years ago and still feels fresh today, but you are not required to keep reliving what God is trying to release you from. I encourage you to forgive and let it go.

You cannot move forward in life holding on to old hurts. Walking in unforgiveness is like carrying around spoiled garbage through every room of your life. The longer you continue to keep it, the worse the stench becomes.

It seeps into your conversations. It shows up in your relationships. It affects your peace. And whether you intend to or not, it impacts everyone around you. Forgive and allow God to fumigate the situation. Let Him cleanse the air of your heart.

And while you're at it, forgive yourself. Be kind to yourself. Extend the same grace you so freely give to others. Forgiveness is not just about them, but it is also for you. I'm not saying it will erase what happened or that you'll even forget about it, but it will remove you from the holding pattern of shame and regret.

The scars may even still be there, but they are not reminders of failure or loss. They are proof that you survived. They are signs of victory and overcoming.

Starting today, look at yourself in the mirror and say, *"I forgive you for that mistake. I forgive you for choosing others over you. I forgive you for not listening to the voice of God."* Speak it aloud so that your ears hear what your heart needs.

And then, if you can't directly confront whomever or whatever else that hurt you, release it in prayer with a pure heart and the right intent. Forgive yourself freely

Good Morning.

and the spirit you allowed to use you.

Today is your day of liberty. I celebrate your entry into the abundance that has been waiting for you on the other side of this release. Moving forward in forgiveness is not easy, but today, you are taking the first bold step toward the life you've been praying for. Those ill feelings you feel will soon be replaced with God's divine love, unshakeable joy and lasting peace. Keep forgiving. Keep releasing. Keep moving forward.

You are free.

Good Morning.

Reflect

Ephesians 4:31-32 Get rid of all bitterness, rage and anger, brawling and slander, along with every form of malice. Be kind and compassionate to one another, forgiving each other, just as in Christ God forgave you.

Matthew 6:14-15 For if you forgive other people when they sin against you, your heavenly Father will also forgive you. But if you do not forgive others their sins, your Father will not forgive your sins.

Isaiah 43:25 "I, even I, am he who blots out your transgressions, for my own sake, and remembers your sins no more."

Colossians 3:13 Bear with each other and forgive one another if any of you has a grievance against someone. Forgive as the Lord forgave you.

Today, I forgive...

Love Yourself Unconditionally

Have you ever stopped to tell yourself, "I love you!"—and actually mean it? Not casually. Not jokingly. But intentionally. Boldy. With conviction. Then, list all the things you love about yourself—your resilience, your compassion, your creativity, your growth. It is essential that the love you wish to receive from and even reciprocate to others must first begin with you loving yourself.

Yes, life has a way of testing our confidence. It's true that we can go through so much and even be told so many negative things that we start to question our identity, our value, our purpose and our worth. But let me encourage you today that the only perspective that has authority over your life is God's. If He can love you unconditionally, then why can't you love yourself the same?

There was a time I used to worry about what people said and thought about me. I gave their voices too much power until, one day, I stopped to reevaluate who those people were in my life and their reputation.

Then, I was reminded that no matter what they said or thought about me, God's hand was still upon me. Their chatter could not cancel His calling. Their opinions could not block His blessings. I realized I didn't need their approval because God loved and continues to love me unconditionally.

So this morning, I encourage you to look at yourself in the mirror. Say your name, and declare, "*I love you*" and really mean it. Today, I look at myself in the mirror and say, "Kitta, I LOVE YOU—flaws and all." No, I'm not perfect, but God is still doing a perfect work within me!

Once you come into agreement with what God says about you and boldly believe and speak it too, you will begin to see an elevation in your thought-patterns, the company you keep, what you are attracted to and what you attract. All aspects of your life will start to align with your new level of self-worth. Loving yourself isn't arrogance—it's alignment.

Good Morning.

I'm not just learning to love who I am. I'm falling in love with who I'm becoming—this new version of me. And when you truly love yourself through God's lens, you step into a freedom no opinion can shake and no circumstance can steal.

Good Morning.

Song of Songs 4:7 You are altogether beautiful, my darling; there is no flaw in you.

Ephesians 2:10 For we are God's handiwork, created in Christ Jesus to do good works, which God prepared in advance for us to do.

Today, I love the fact that I...

Day 9

Rest

Sometimes you may find yourself mentally busy to the point of exhaustion. In your mind, you're doing 50 million things but executing nothing. When you make the slightest move to do something, you're completely wiped out. Your body is trying to tell you that you need rest.

When I was juggling my roles as a worship leader at church, independent artist on the road, Kurt Carr singer on tour and mommy all day, every day, I was being pulled in so many different directions. My mind was so overwhelmed with all the responsibilities that I felt like I couldn't do anything. In fact, I didn't want to do anything because I was feeling unfulfilled. I was simply burnt out. I needed to rest.

For clarity's sake, when I say rest, I'm not just speaking of a "chill" day or period of doing nothing. I am speaking of a time for you to turn the brain off, inhale, exhale and think about nothing. Relinquish control and go with the flow. What's meant to be and happen for your life will make its way to you according to the energy you release and the belief system you maintain.

Don't overload your mental space so much that it adds unnecessary stress to your physical well-being. Don't overthink your way out of embracing potential wins, victories, come-ups, connections or promotions. Resting gives you a clearer outlook on life so that you can do all that you are called to do.

Here are 10 practical ways you can rest:

- Take a 5-10 minute no-response break. No phone, no talking, just sitting.

- Do a brain dump in which you write everything on your mind on paper.

- Step outside for fresh air without multitasking.

- Try short breathing exercises. Inhale for 4 seconds. Hold for 4 seconds. Exhale for 6 seconds.

Good Morning.

- Take a power nap for no more than 25 minutes. I love this so much. My kind of carrying on…LOL

- Go to bed earlier—even 30 minutes helps.

- Turn off notifications for a while. (DND)

- Sit in your car and just be for a few minutes before going inside.

- Listen to music that moves you. I have a few projects that can help. #shamelessplug

- Go for a walk in nature or look at something beautiful.

Remember, if it drains you, limit it. If it restores you, prioritize it. Now, rest your mind. Then go to work!

Good Morning.

I Peter 5:7 Cast all your anxiety on him because he cares for you.

Matthew 6:34 Therefore, do not worry about tomorrow, for tomorrow will will worry about itself. Each day has enough trouble of its own.

Mathew 11:28-30 Then Jesus said, *"Come to me, all of you who are weary and carry heavy burdens, and I will give you rest."*

Today, I will rest my mind by...

Day 10

Reexamine Yourself

As the phrase in Psalm 63:1 goes, "Early will I seek Thee," but lately God's been coming after me….4 a.m. really, God? LOL…It's okay because I'm learning that when God interrupts our comfort, it's often because He wants our attention. And when He has our attention, He has something to say.

This morning, I am excited about our time together because God shared some nuggets of wisdom with me. The first step towards getting it right is confession. For whatever reason, we never want to admit that we've been the problem or even have a problem. We cannot grow if we refuse to admit where we've been wrong. We can't be so self-centered to think that we're always right and have never been the one with the issue.

If we step back and honestly reexamine ourselves, we should quickly realize that we are not perfect. And the good news is we don't have to live in denial, and the mistakes we make don't always have to be repeated.

Then, God asked me, *"Who are you connected to?"* Do they live the life you desire? Do their actions align with their words? Do you all learn and grow from each other?

If you're more accomplished or grounded than most of the company you keep, then how can you expect to grow? What and who you surround yourself with is low-key who and what you become.

What conversations are you entertaining? What goals do you all discuss? How have they made you a better person? Remember, purposeful connections produce progress. Don't allow your associations with small-minded people keep you in bondage!

Then He cautioned, *"So either you can make the necessary changes, or you can continue in your own ways, repeating the same cycles."* You can continue feeling frustrated, depressed and or dejected as a result of the repeated choices you make. Or, you can learn from your mistakes and move forward in life.

Good Morning.

Wow! It's a teary morning today, but I'm crying tears of joy. I'm shedding these tears because we have decided to grow—reexamine ourselves, realign our connections and refuse to stay stagnant.

I'm excited about our journey together, and I want to encourage you to take the necessary time and steps to reexamining yourself and becoming the best YOU—one who cannot be denied by anyone or anything. It's a great day already!

Good Morning.

1 John 1:9 If we confess our sins, he is faithful and just and will forgive us our sins and purify us from all unrighteousness.

1 Corinthians 15:33 Do not be misled: "Bad company corrupts good character."

Proverbs 13:20 Walk with the wise and become wise, for a companion of fools suffers harm.

Proverbs 27:17 As iron sharpens iron, so one person sharpens another.

Romans 12:2 Do not conform to the pattern of this world, but be transformed by the renewing of your mind. Then you will be able to test and approve what God's will is—his good, pleasing and perfect will.

Today, I reexamine myself and my connections and realize that...

Protect Your Peace

Understand and know that we have to really be careful of the assignments we assume. We have to be very cognizant of who and what we attach ourselves to. Everyone and everything are not meant to always consume our time, heart and energy. Not every situation is ours to fix, and not every person is ours to carry.

Yes, I understand your pure heart and motive will cause you to gravitate to what looks like could use your help. But you must also understand that people and their situations can only be helped if they realize they need the help and are willing to put in the work to get it.

Too often, we rush to rescue others from a place of compassion but never stop to think about some difficult realities. The hurt almost always hurt others. The conflicted rarely know how to resolve conflict. The insecure will find a way to knock you down. And the entitled will only expect to receive without ever giving.

I'm not saying we shouldn't attempt to help them. We just need to know our limits as to how far we should engage. We must establish healthy boundaries to protect our peace. It's okay to walk away once you've realized a situation is beyond your capacity of support.

Setting healthy boundaries preserves your peace. They act like gatekeepers around it, ensuring that what enters your life aligns with your purpose, values and well-being. Without them, we oftentimes say "yes" when we really want to say "no." Over time, we become frustrated, bitter and emotionally burnt out.

By setting healthy boundaries, you allow your "yes" to mean "yes" and your "no" to mean "no." In case you did not know, your "no" is a complete sentence by itself —no explanation, justification nor apology needed.

People can easily overstep, placing their expectations, problems and negativity on you. If you're not careful, you can end up carrying burdens that were never yours to bear.

Good Morning.

Setting healthy boundaries empowers you to decide what you will carry and what you must release. By doing so, you conserve the emotional and spiritual energy needed for the things that truly matter in your life. Many times, I've had to tell myself, "It's no longer my assignment!"

There's a line from an old hymn that says, "Oh what peace we often forfeit and oh what needless pain we bear." I believe this happens when we refuse to take our hands off and walk away from situations that drain us emotionally, mentally, spiritually and even financially.

If it makes you feel some type of way, wastes your time or makes you question the person you know you are, quit fooling with it. Your peace is valuable, and you've got to do all within your power to protect it daily. Every battle is not yours to fight, and every burden is not yours to bear. Peace comes when you begin to recognize it's simply no longer your assignment.

Good Morning.

Reflect

2 Thessalonians 3:10-13 For even when we were with you, we gave you this rule: "The one who is unwilling to work shall not eat."

Proverbs 13:20 Walk with the wise and become wise, for a companion of fools suffers harm.

Proverbs 4:23 Above all else, guard your heart, for everything you do flows from it.

Isaiah 26:3 You will keep in perfect peace those whose minds are steadfast, because they trust in you.

Colossians 3:15 Let the peace of Christ rule in your hearts, since as members of one body you were called to peace. And be thankful.

Today, my boundary will be...

____

____

____

____

____

____

____

____

Keep Moving!

This morning, I woke up thinking this isn't happening fast enough. I've been grinding hard for years—working, praying, planning, doing everything I know to do—but I just don't feel like I'm making any progress. I've tried to check off all the boxes of what I think I should be doing to reach my goals, but it feels like I'm stuck in a rut—like I'm moving but somehow not getting anywhere.

And then, in the stillness of the morning, God spoke to me and said, *"Just keep moving! Don't get distracted by time. Don't get discouraged by what you don't see yet. You already know where you're going, and you have all you need to reach your destination. Just keep moving!"*

Many times, we never fully accomplish our goals in life because we become discouraged in the process. We get tired of waiting and become anxious for immediate results. I've been there many times.

That's usually when the trap of comparison appears. We begin to compare ourselves to others, which is a huge no-no. What once felt like forward motion suddenly feels like failure. We may have started off great in the process, but, once we begin to compare our progress to others, we become disappointed in ourselves. We begin to feel like that old car sitting on the side of the road while everyone else speeds past.

The grass may look greener on the other side, but can you afford the water bill? In other words, you may not know the sacrifices that person had to make to reach their goals and maintain their success. And you may not even be willing to endure the struggles and hardships they had to overcome to get to where they are. Be careful when you begin to compare yourself to others because, as Theodore Roosevelt often said, comparison really is the thief of joy.

This morning, I want to encourage you to not let what you see in the natural disrupt what's been assigned to you in the spirit! It may not look like anything is happening, but it is. Seeds grow underground long before anyone sees the harvest.

Good Morning.

Your destiny depends on you because only you can move you! It reminds me of the blue arrow on my GPS, which I use on the regular. Whether I know the route or not, that blue arrow guides me step by step towards my destination. If I don't move, neither does that blue arrow move. Everything is at a standstill. But when I keep pressing ahead, so does that blue arrow too—turn by turn, mile by mile—until, eventually, I arrive.

Life works the same way. Progress doesn't always come in leaps. Sometimes, it comes in faithful steps. As the Chinese proverb goes, "The journey of 1,000 miles begins with a single step." So continue stepping. Keep moving! God has great things ahead. Gotta go and get it!

Good Morning.

Galatians 6:9 Let us not become weary in doing good, for at the proper time we will reap a harvest if we do not give up.

Proverbs 3:5-6 Trust the LORD with all your heart and lean not on your own understanding; in all your ways submit to him, and he will make your paths straight.

Today, I will...

Care for Your Children

During my quiet time this morning, I was reminded of how crucial it is as a parent to constantly pray for our children—lifting them up, encouraging them, and always being mindful of the people and influences we allow into their space. Children are like sponges, absorbing everything around them, even the things we think they don't notice.

I can't help but reflect on the responsibility I have in shaping my children's world. In everything I do, I must always think about how it would affect them.

For single mothers, especially when choosing a mate, it's important to ask yourself some honest questions: *Is this someone I'd be comfortable having around my daughter? Is this someone she could respect or even feel proud to see me with?* And for my son, am I carrying myself in a way that will elevate the type of woman he will one day choose?

I realize that more is caught than taught. Our children are watching everything we say and do. They are studying how we respond to life, how we handle challenges, how we love and how we lead.

Do they see us pray? Do they witness peace in our homes? Do they feel loved, protected and safe? Do they know they can trust us to be present when they need us?

We are their first examples of life, love, discipline, faith and leadership. Long before the world starts to shape them, we do. So much of who they become begins with us.

As parents, we must be intentional. I challenge myself—and every parent—to pray with our children each morning, especially before school. Ask them what they expect from their day and encourage them to declare that it will be a great one. Teach them early that their words have power and their mindset matters.

Then, in the evenings, when they return home, take a moment to ask how their

Good Morning.

day went. What were the highlights? What could have made the day even better? These simple conversations of connection build trust, strengthen relationships and let them know their voice matters.

Let's also make time for the little things that mean so much—doing chores together, enjoying movie or game nights or even cooking together as a family. Reward them when they deserve it, and correct them when they are wrong. Both are necessary for growth.

Even if you aren't a parent, your influence matters. The young people around you—your nieces, nephews, little cousins and even neighborhood kids—are watching too. Never underestimate the impact you have on a child's life. Oh the many great lessons I learned from my mentors and those I watched from afar!

Within the twinkling of an eye, our children will grow up to become adults—leaders, bosses, managers, teachers and so much more. What will they carry with them from us?

It is our responsibility and privilege to help shape them and mold them into someone we will one day look at with pride. When you positively impact a child's life, you are doing more than just raising a child. You are building a brighter future.

Good Morning.

Reflect

Proverbs 22:6 Start children off on the way they should go, and even when they are old they will not turn from it.

Isaiah 54:13 All your children will be taught by the Lord, and great will be their peace.

Psalm 127:3-5 Children are a heritage from the Lord, offspring a reward from him. Like arrows In the hands of a warrior are children born in one's youth. Blessed is the man whose quiver is full of them. They will not be put to shame when they contend with their opponents in court.

Today, I will make sure my child...

____

____

____

____

____

____

____

Day 14

Glorify God

I've always tried to be there for everyone. I've worked hard to preserve my relationships as a parent, sibling, relative, employee, significant other and friend. But if I'm honest, there have been moments when discouragement tried to creep in.

There have been times when the love and support I wished to have received (and sometimes even needed) didn't come from the people and places I expected it to. And that was a hard reality to accept.

I've always felt that the place where you pour and even empty your heart should also be the same place that refills you, the place that uplifts you, the place that shows you the most love. Surely the principle of reciprocity must be true. You are supposed to get out of something what you put into it.

I tried not to get discouraged, feeling as though I was being undervalued, unappreciated or flat out used, but at the same time, seeing, hearing and feeling the love from those places can give you the boost to keep working harder. It would make you not mind pouring your all into it.

But then God had to check me. He prompted me to question my motives. *Who are you pouring for? Why are you pouring? Is it with the right intention? Is it really for them or for your own glory?*

Then suddenly, I asked the Lord to check my heart first. All I do should be unto Him—to glorify His Name and then be a help to others. That realignment was so needed because it helped me to shift my mindset and focus.

When your purpose becomes glorifying God instead of seeking validation from people, your perspective changes. You're no longer controlled by the applause or discouraged by the silence. Your focus becomes higher and your motivation purer.

Good Morning.

Our ultimate purpose in life should always be to glorify God—not self or man. Yes, we are human with emotions and feelings, but we can't let them lead us. Sometimes we have to refocus our focus and remember why we started in the first place.

You may be in a situation feeling how I felt, but when you begin to free yourself from seeking validation from people and begin to glorify God, He begins to move in ways you never expected.

Just like God, He'll send all you need from the most unexpected places. What's crazy is I had been seeking love and support from one place, but God delivered it through another—total strangers who reminded me I am seen, loved and supported.

Wow! We should never limit God. Don't put Him in a box. Don't assume the blessing has to come through the door you're watching. It may not come from where you want it, but it's coming!

Just keep pouring. Keep serving. Keep showing up. And above all, keep giving God all the glory.

Good Morning.

Reflect

Hebrews 6:10 God is not unjust; he will not forget your work and the love you have shown him as you have helped his people and continue to help them.

Psalm 139:23–24 Search me, God, and know my heart; test me and know my anxious thoughts. See if there is any offensive way in me, and lead me in the way everlasting.

Galations 6:9 Let us not become weary in doing good, for at the proper time we will reap a harvest if we do not give up.

Today, I will glorify...

____

____

____

____

____

____

Listen to Your Body

This morning, I thought about times I kept going and going and going because my responsibilities would not allow me to rest—making sure my kids were straight, serving in various leadership roles at the church, traveling as an artist for events, trying to keep a consistent workout schedule and the list goes on. My days were packed, and my nights were short. I was juggling so many roles that five or six hours of sleep felt normal—sometimes less than that!

Do you realize, the older we become, the harder it is to maintain this kind of lifestyle? Over time, your body begins to whisper. You start to feel and notice changes you hadn't felt before. Many of us get those warning signs, but we choose to ignore them.

We keep pushing and pushing thinking nothing about the swollen ankle, lingering stomach pain or strange sensation in the back of our throat. We push through the discomfort, convincing ourselves we'll deal with it later. Sometimes we may even go all day without eating a proper meal.

Then, one day, against our own will, our body physically shuts down. We can't go any further. We need to rest and are forced to deal with the sickness that might have been prevented if we had only listened earlier. We should have given our body the proper care and essential nutrients needed to keep it going.

If we think about a car, there are certain things it needs for it to perform according to its design. Oil for the engine, gas for the tank and air in the tires are just a few of the basic necessities. When my car is low on any of those essentials, I receive system alerts and am forced to stop and take care of it. Our bodies work the same way.

These days, I often joke and say, "Whew! Now that I'm 50, my check engine light stays on." LOL. I am always monitoring various aspects of my health because when my body talks, I listen. But there was a time when I didn't, and things could have gone another way.

Good Morning.

I remember a few years ago I was having a series of excruciating headaches. Instead of slowing down, I kept going, taking ibuprofen, Advil or whatever I could find to give me some relief. One Sunday, the pain became so unbearable that I left the sanctuary feeling dizzy and weak. One of the nurses in the congregation suggested checking my blood pressure, and the results were alarming.

My blood pressure had elevated to stroke-level numbers. The headaches I was ignoring were symptoms of chronic hypertension, and I thank God we were able to address the situation before something worse could have happened. That experience taught me that ignoring your body does not make the warning signs disappear. It only makes the consequences louder.

We can do many things to pursue a healthy lifestyle. We can schedule regular doctor visits, drink more water to stay hydrated, squeeze in some cardio to keep that heart pumping and blood flowing and consume a healthy diet to fuel our energy. But none of those things truly matter if we do not first listen to the very body we're trying to care for.

If something feels off, don't ignore it. It will not just go away. Take heed to it and respond accordingly. A small neglect today could have negative life-changing repercussions tomorrow. I chose to live because I want to live a long prosperous, meaningful life in good health.

Good Morning.

Reflect

1 Corinthians 6:19–20 Do you not know that your bodies are temples of the Holy Spirit, who is in you, whom you have received from God? You are not your own; you were bought at a price. Therefore honor God with your bodies.

Today, my body is saying...

Affirm Yourself Daily

Believe it or not, words have power. We often hear people telling each other, "I love you to death." Although this expression shows strong compassion for someone, the outcome is undesirable. We don't want our loved ones to die. We want them to live. So, let's shift that narrative. Let's start saying, "I love you to life."

Then, it occurred to me. Have we ever been intentional about loving ourselves to life?

Freedom doesn't begin when someone else validates you. It starts when you decide you are worthy of your own love. Loving yourself to life means loving yourself out of bondage to the negative thoughts or actions of others. It means loving yourself enough to recognize how you deserve to be treated and holding those accountable when they fall short.

You should love yourself enough to know what you deserve and have the courage to walk away from any situation that doesn't suit you. Love yourself enough to chase and cherish peace. Love yourself enough to forgive yourself for the seasons when you did not always see the best in you or believe the best for you.

You don't have to wait for others to tell you what they love about you, although I'll admit it's always nice to hear. Let's normalize affirming our own selves daily by speaking life over ourselves when we look at ourselves in the mirror. Don't just stop at the outer but look deep within to tell yourself what you love about YOU!

So today, I need your participation. Affirm yourself each day, appreciating the positive qualities you possess. Not arrogantly. Not superficially. Not hesitantly. But honestly.

I'll start because I've really been loving me to life!

What I LOVE about me.....

Good Morning.

I love that I'm beautiful, and the same beauty within matches what you see outwardly.

I love my dimples because what's considered a defect makes a picture-perfect smile.

I love my eyes because they are bright and sincere.

I love that I'm strong yet gentle enough to be soft when the situation requires it.

I love that I'm a survivor and can literally bounce back from anything.

I love that I can enjoy my own company and not depend on anyone else to complete my joy.

I love that I'm loyal and trustworthy. (Just learning to balance my loyalty and trust with boundaries now)

I love that I'm a natural leader.

I love my versatility.

Wow! I could go on and on, but I'll stop here for now. I'm so loving me, and it's giving me so much life!

Loving yourself to life changes the way you give love and the way you receive it. When you affirm yourself daily, you stop accepting crumbs or apologizing for the bright light that radiates all around you.

Now, it's your turn. During your journal time, tell me what you love about you. Don't rush it. Don't overthink it. Just let it flow. Affirm yourself daily because you've only got one YOU to LOVE.

Good Morning.

Proverbs 12:25 Anxiety weighs down the heart, but a kind word cheers it up.

Psalm 139:14 I will praise you, for I am fearfully and wonderfully made.

Romans 8:1 There is therefore now no condemnation for those who are in Christ Jesus.

Today, I love that I...

____

____

____

____

____

____

Be Grateful

This morning, my time was filled with nothing but gratitude. I didn't ask God for one thing. I just let it be known that I am super grateful for everything. The more I thanked Him, the more my heart began to overflow with gratitude. More and more reasons came to mind as to why I was so grateful.

Thank You God for my life. Thank You God for my health and strength. Thank You God for my children. Thank You God for sanity. Thank You God for my gifts. Thank You God for my connection to You.

When my children express their appreciation for things I do for them, it encourages me to want to do more. Instead of hearing them complain about what they don't have or what they "need," a simple unsolicited "Thank You, Mommy" goes a long way. And it doesn't even have to be in response to material gifts. Them simply being grateful for the essential things I provide as a mother fills my heart with joy.

Then, I thought, "What if God, our Heavenly Father, felt the same way about us, His children?" What if we started our day thanking God for the simple things in life.

I know it may sound cliché, but what if we simply thanked Him for the breath in our lungs, the ability to see, hear, taste, smell and move? What if we thanked Him for having a sound mind? Wouldn't He not want to bless us even more because we thanked Him for the "little things" we often neglect?

Now, I'm not saying that we should thank Him with the intent of receiving more blessings. All I'm saying is that, instead of focusing on the lack in our lives, we must learn to appreciate the blessings we already have.

Your life, even with its challenges, holds gifts someone else is praying for. There is always somebody who would love to be in your shoes, and your situation could always be much worse.

Good Morning.

I know I have access to everything because my Father owns it all. However, it's His choice to bless continually. It is His choice to give me the resources—His choice to even give me the wisdom to know the things I need and the ability to obtain them. Any way you look at it today, I'm grateful that He continues to be mindful of me.

Don't jumpstart your day complaining about the who's, the what's, the when's and the how's of your life. Simply be grateful for everything. I think I'll go listen to my song, *Grateful*.

Have an AMAZING day!

Good Morning.

Psalm 9:1 I will give thanks to you, LORD, with all my heart; I will tell of all your wonderful deeds.

Psalm 107:1 Give thanks to the LORD, for he is good; his love endures forever.

Today, I thank God for...

Day 18

Become Your Best Self

There is no embarrassment in failure. It's okay to mess up or lose your way sometimes—every meaningful journey includes a few wrong turns. Many people have stood exactly where you are, faced setbacks but never found the courage to rise again.

I challenge you to find your way by fixing what you can, learning what you must and keep moving forward. Failure is not a mark of shame; it's evidence that you dared to try.

Your growth and progress may never be seen, acknowledged or even understood by others. And that's perfectly okay. Be okay with that as long as you see the difference.

Celebrate yourself for the work you put into building a better version of you. Be your loudest screamer, hardest clapper and the dopest hype-person on your team. Be your own cheerleader! Go YOU! You're doing better than you think.

Your peace is something you create. We do ourselves a huge disservice when we allow our peace to be determined by who comes and goes in and out of our lives. Obtaining real peace starts from within.

I now cringe at the statement we often hear, "Be his/her peace." How about we encourage them to find their own peace? Finding your own peace means abandoning all the expectations and desires you place on others to fix you, love you, and make you happy. Take responsibility for your own healing and happiness because, once you experience true peace, no one can take that away from you.

Being "selfish" in the right way can actually be one of the most selfless things you do. When you constantly pour into everyone else but neglect yourself, you rob the world—and your family—of the best version of you. The best version of you would never emerge to be the best for those who need it! Some of you will understand this later.

Good Morning.

I'm truly working on something because I'm looking forward to something. The better I am, the better quality of life for my kids. I absolutely am in love with who I'm becoming! It's about me, and it's for me—and it blesses everyone around me.

Good Morning.

Reflect

Proverbs 24:16 The godly may trip seven times, but they will get up again. But one disaster is enough to overthrow the wicked.

Philippians 4:4-7 Rejoice in the Lord always. I say it again: Rejoice! Let your gentleness be evident to all. The Lord is near. Do not be anxious about anything, but in every situation, by prayer and petition, with thanksgiving, present your requests to God. And the peace of God, which transcends all understanding, will guard your hearts and your minds in Christ Jesus.

Romans 15:13 May the God of hope fill you with all joy and peace as you trust in him, so that you may overflow with hope by the power of the Holy Spirit.

Today, I will become my best self by...

Be Kind to Others

Real talk this morning. As I reflect on my 51 years of living, I can honestly say I have survived some of my toughest days and darkest nights. I have attempted to unalive (as they say now) myself several times because I was so unsure of myself. I wondered if I would be able to overcome and bounce back from various circumstances. I questioned if things would get better. There were so many thoughts clouding my mind that committing suicide seemed to be the best alternative.

Before I ever reached this depth of despair, I used to wonder how anyone could take their own life. I would often tell myself, "I'd never do that!" But life has a way of humbling us. It teaches us that we can't always predict how we'll respond when we're pushed to our emotional and spiritual limits.

We each have our own levels of faith, strength and resilience that build us up, but, sometimes, we can reach a low so low that we give up and break. We momentarily lose sight of the way out.

If you saw me in public during those seasons, you'd never know my private battle —whether to live or die—because I always came outside looking as if I was living my best life. Hair done. Face beat. Clothes fashionable. Nails flawless and a look that always attracted compliments.

Many would often tell me how beautiful and glamorous I looked. But deep down inside, I felt like a dead woman walking. Broken, exhausted and barely holding on.

Today, I'm grateful that those dark moments didn't fully consume me. I'm thankful I am still here to share a snippet of my story. And through my survival, life has taught me a couple of powerful truths.

First, never judge a person's decisions based on a situation you've never experienced. You may try to empathize, but until you've carried the exact weight they are carrying, you cannot fully understand their struggle. Some battles take

Good Morning.

longer to overcome than others.

What may look like weakness from the outside could actually be someone fighting with everything they have to just keep going. So extend patience. Extend grace. Don't be so quick to judge and condemn someone who is simply trying to come up and out of their dark place.

Secondly, understand that a person's outward appearance does not always reflect how he/she is functioning on the inside. Many of us walk around through life wearing carefully crafted masks, pretending to be okay when we are outright miserable. There are silent battles happening deep within we do not dare to share. Therefore, it is important to be kind to everyone whether you think it's needed or not.

Even the strongest person in your circle may need a kind word. Even the friend who always encourages everyone else may secretly need encouragement themselves.

Take the time to ask them, *"Are you okay? No, really…are you okay?"* Then, say things that build them up as opposed to tearing them down. Sometimes a simple gesture, a sincere compliment or a moment of genuine care can be the very thing that helps someone find the strength to keep pressing forward.

I haven't always had it all "together," and I'm grateful to those who showed me patience when I was struggling. Their affirming words, selfless deeds and countless prayers helped carry me through moments when I couldn't carry myself.

So instead of ridiculing or shaming someone who may be in a dark season, simply be kind to others. I'm so grateful others were kind to me so that I could live to tell the story!

Psalm 34:19 The righteous person may have many troubles, but the LORD delivers him from them all.

Galatians 6:2 Carry each other's burdens, and in this way you will fulfill the law of Christ.

Psalm 147:3 He heals the brokenhearted and binds up their wounds.

Colossians 3:12 Therefore, as God's chosen people, holy and dearly loved, clothe yourselves with compassion, kindness, humility, gentleness and patience.

Today, I will be kind to...

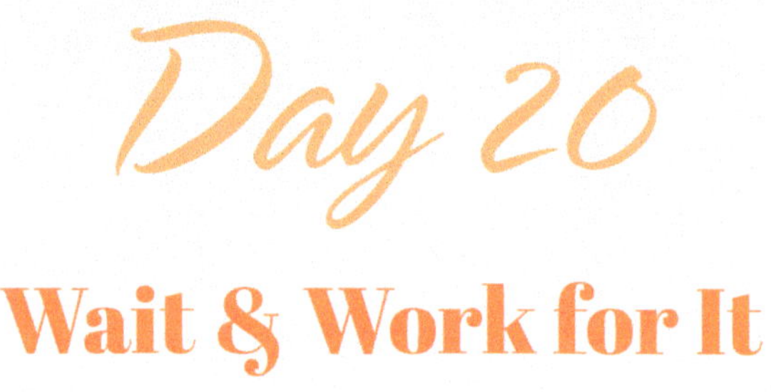

Wait & Work for It

What does your wait-time look like? It's a serious question. Oftentimes, we forfeit a favorable outcome because we don't know how to handle the meantime, in between time. The weight of the wait can feel unbearable.

Most of us fill our wait-time doubting, questioning, wondering, and actually creating more stress than necessary. Instead of wallowing in the wait, we should fill our waiting season with work, study, practice, planning, preparation, prayer, reflection and course correction.

It's not enough to just ask God for something and then take no steps toward it. Waiting doesn't mean doing nothing. It takes more than just having faith. As mentioned in James 2:26, faith without works is dead. Faith requires movement.

Imagine being a waiter, and even though the title may suggest someone who waits, the job requires more than just that. A waiter is someone who serves and is in constant motion. His/her quality of service (diligence) determines the quantity of tips (overflow). The better he/she "waits," the greater the reward.

So even during the wait season, you have to work your faith preparing for the "it" to manifest. And even when it finally happens, you still must put in the work to maintain it or risk losing it.

When we properly learn how to wait and what to do during the wait, our true purpose comes faster than we could have imagined without all the unnecessary drama. I thank God He has allowed me to see what's done in waiting (the process) is more important than what's done when it arrives (the promise).

What feels like delay is often development. Who would have thought the amount of time I sang background for Kurt Carr was preparing me to launch my career as an independent artist.

So guard your waiting season. Fill your time with positive things that are important to you and for you—things that will grow you, prosper you, heal you,

Good Morning.

bring you joy and position you for greatness. An idle mind is definitely open territory for the enemy to slide in and destroy all the focus, momentum, creativity, and excitement you've created thus far. Don't play with it!

Stay on your job focusing on those things because the enemy—whomever or whatever that looks like for you—isn't gonna let up! The same energy the enemy uses to try and defeat you should be the same level of energy you use to stay committed to becoming better.

Learn how to properly wait, and watch what happens when the "it" manifests. Even when it feels like nothing is happening, God is working things out on your behalf. Sit back. Wait—and work for it. Okay? Remember God is still in the midst of it all because He has not forgotten about you!

Good Morning.

Isaiah 40:27-31 Why do you complain, Jacob? Why do you say, Israel, "My way is hidden from the LORD; my cause is disregarded by my God"? Do you not know? Have you not heard? The LORD is the everlasting God, the Creator of the ends of the earth. He will not grow tired or weary, and his understanding no one can fathom. He gives strength to the weary and increases the power of the weak. Even youths grow tired and weary, and young men stumble and fall; but those who hope in the LORD will renew their strength. They will soar on wings like eagles; they will run and not grow weary, they will walk and not be faint.

Today, during my wait season, I will work on...

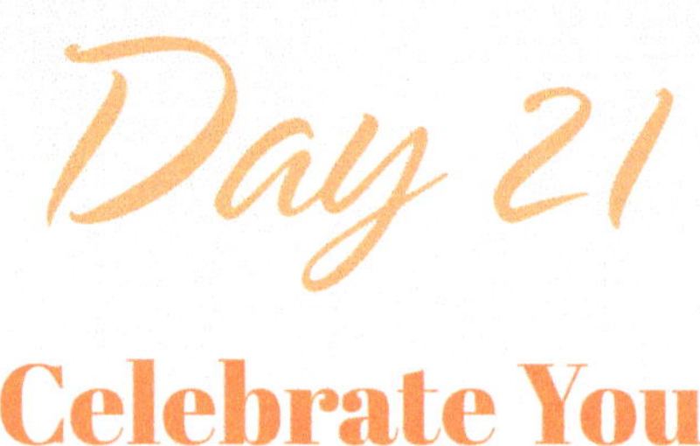

Celebrate You

When I woke up this morning, the first thing I did was give God praise. But right after that, I did something just as powerful. I took a moment to celebrate myself.

I celebrated the work I've put in and the growth I've experienced. I celebrated me for being more concerned with what I look like to God and to myself rather than what I look like to others. That kind of freedom is priceless.

I celebrated my consistency and staying focused when distractions tried to pull me away. I celebrated the decisions I made that were best for me—choices that protected my peace, strengthened my character and aligned me with my purpose.

I celebrated me being an amazing woman and even more so an amazing mother. I celebrated the fact that I've overcome obstacles that the average person would not have survived. I celebrated my private victories, ones that no one may ever know. I even celebrated upcoming successes that you will see and maybe even celebrate with me. Yes, I had a great pat-yourself-on-the-back moment with myself!

I share all of this to say that you've got to learn how to throw yourself your own victory party. If God sees our victories and rejoices over us, why can't we do the same for ourselves?

Too often, we wait, seek and hope for validation and congrats from others, but the truth is those people don't want to see you win and will never celebrate you. And some only want you to succeed if it somehow benefits them.

You've worked hard. You've accomplished more than you realize. Boldly tell yourself, "I did that, and I will keep achieving!"

Every time you pause to recognize something you did well—no matter how small —you strengthen your belief in your ability to succeed. Your confidence grows when you acknowledge your progress. And building that confidence over time

Good Morning.

reshapes your mindset from doubt to belief. It keeps you motivated and reminds you that progress is happening even when you haven't reached the destination yet.

As much as we are our harshest critics, we can easily throw ourselves our own pity party. Woe is me for this, and woe is me for that. But today is not about focusing on what's going wrong in our lives. I encourage you to recognize what's going well—no matter how insignificant it may seem.

Just think about it. You've got a lot to celebrate about yourself. Every single day you're becoming someone stronger. Every single day you're becoming wiser. Every single day you're becoming more fulfilled along the journey. Nothing can stop you.

So celebrate yourself today. Applaud your growth and honor your journey. No matter what's going on in your life, never forget to celebrate you! You go boy! You go girl!

Good Morning.

Galatians 6:4 Each one should test their own actions. Then they can take pride in themselves alone, without comparing themselves to someone else.

Philippians 1:6 Being confident of this, that He who began a good work in you will carry it on to completion until the day of Christ Jesus.

Ecclesiastes 3:13 That each of them may eat and drink, and find satisfaction in all their toil—this is the gift of God.

Philippians 4:4 Rejoice in the Lord always. I will say it again: Rejoice!

Today, I celebrate that I...

____

____

____

____

____

____

____

From My Heart to Yours

Congratulations! You did it. You completed a 21-day journey to faith, freedom and forward movement. Hopefully, you've become stronger, wiser and better because of this process. I know some mornings may have been difficult to wake up, but you stayed the course and made it to the end. Or shall I say new beginning…Good Morning. (I couldn't resist…LOL 😆)

Now before you go, I want to speak a special blessing over you. May it grant you the breakthrough you desire:

Today, I declare that every crooked place be made straight, every path be cleared and that nothing will hinder your progress. I pray that nothing will cause you to lose focus on the goals that you have set and sought after God to achieve.

I declare that finances will not be a strain on your household or cause you unnecessary stress. I declare that every need is met and even your wants are honored. Your work ethic is increased, and your integrity in the workplace is well spoken of.

I declare that God and good character move to the forefront and, before any works are shown, your lifestyle speaks. I speak unmerited favor over your life. It surrounds you and goes before you—even now, your name is being spoken in rooms you have not entered. Doors are opening on your behalf.

I declare that your children are brilliant geniuses. I declare that learning becomes easy as well as interesting for them and that they are covered and protected everyday. I declare that they don't forget abroad what you've taught them at home. They will always cling to what's good and turn away from the bad.

With the power I've been given to speak what is and cannot be, I call off the bullies assigned to them right now. I speak that a humble spirit will permeate, and the only peer pressure to influence them is the pressure to achieve good grades and even greater conduct. Your

Good Morning.

children are blessed, and they will succeed. They will surpass the odds stacked against them.

I pray that you are a Godly, good example before your children. You make the best decisions for them and in front of them. You love them how the Father loves
us. You not only tell them you love them, but you are big at showing them you love them.

I declare every broken heart be mended, every confused mind be stable and that peace now be your portion and your priority. I pray that joy will abide even in the midst of what could or should be sorrow and sadness.

You are the head and not the tail. You are above and not beneath. You are the lender and not the borrower. You have knowledge and have been given supernatural power. You are strong and wise—wise enough to hear the voice of God and all the wiser to obey Him! No more procrastination! No more fear!

I speak that you trust yourself and the God in you to make the right choices. You align yourself with the right people, places and opportunities that should have access to your space, your light, your heart and soul.

I pray for divine connections and resources to manifest in your life. Let no good thing be withheld from you. May God shine his countenance upon you and grant you unlimited favor. I decree and declare that your light will shine so brightly that all will see the God in you and become examples of His unconditional and unchanging love.

May your business flourish, and may you be flooded with new ideas and creativity. May you be given something fresh to keep you excited about your journey.

In Jesus' Name, Amen.

Good Morning.

Now take a minute to thank God for the journey for this is where we learn and grow.

Be men and women of your word. Period. If we are the righteousness of God that we say, then let that be what everyone else sees!

Say to yourself: Today will be a day of victory and no defeat because of the Greater One who resides within me!

Have a Super Amazing Day!

ABOUT THE AUTHOR

Nakitta C. Foxx (born Nakitta LeAnn Clegg) is a dynamic singer, anointed worship leader, and rising recording artist whose music uplifts, inspires and heals. While growing up in Prattsville, Arkansas, Nakitta began singing at an early age.

When she moved to Texas to attend Prairie View A&M University, she became a member of The Baptist Student Movement (BSM) Choir where she met then BSM director, Adrian Madearis and later joined his group, *Adrian Madearis and God's Anointed People*.

Singing throughout the city with other groups such as *Gary Mayes & New Era*, Nakitta found her church home at The Fountain of Praise. When she joined the Mass Choir and the Praise Team, it wasn't long before she began assisting with Praise and Worship, where she has been an active member and leader for the past 25 years.

In September 2001, while sitting at work, Nakitta received a life-changing phone call from Gospel Legend Kurt Carr, inviting her to sing with his group, The Kurt Carr Singers. Without hesitation, she joined and has been an active member ever since. You may recall her lead vocals on songs like "God Blocked It" and "Spiritual Makeover."

In 2011 and 2024, she released her solo projects, *Let Us Worship* and *He Kept Me: Deluxe Edition.*

Nakitta resides in Houston, Texas with her two children, Aimee Morgan and Ace Maddox. Wherever she goes, she continues spreading the Good News to bring hope, healing and wholeness to the world.

NAKITTA FOXX

Let's Stay Connected!